Banishing, Binding, Cursing & Hexing

BY
E.M. FAIRCHILDE

About the Author

I have a Bachelor of Science degree in Psychology, but the darker side of the science appealed to me more. Paranormal psychology fascinates me to this day. Metaphysical theories have interested me most of my life and led me to begin studying and using Wiccan concepts several years ago. I consider myself an eclectic, solitary, even chaotic witch, and live with my family, my cat Lola, and one very stubborn Basset Hound named Fritz.

Contact

emfairchilde@gmail.com

I dedicate this book to beginner witches everywhere!

The Magic Is Within You

Non-Fiction Books by E. M. Fairchilde

Book of Shadows, Beginner's Guide,
Information & Workbook
Moon Phase Rituals Made Easy, Beginner's
Guide & Workbook
Sabats and Esbats, Beginner's Guide
Banishing, Binding, Cursing, & Hexing,
Beginner's Guide

Beginner Books Coming Soon
What Kind of *Witch* are You¿
Centering, Grounding & Shielding, Beginner's
Guide
The Elements, Beginner's Guide
The Colors of Magic…White, Black & Gray
Sigils & Chaos Magic, Beginner's Guide
Goddess Magic & Energy, Beginner's Guide
Energize your Magic using Candles, Herbs, Oils
& Stones, Beginner's Guide
The Beginner Witch's Collection Book One
The Beginner Witch's Collection Book Two
Covens, Circles, Groups & Gatherings,
Beginner's Guide
The Beginner Witch's Collection Book Three
Altars, Circles & Sacred Spaces, Beginner's
Guide

Spells, Incantations, Invocations, Evocations &
Rituals, Beginner's Guide
Calling the Quarters, Beginner's Guide
Talismans, Amulets, Lucky Charms & Symbols,
Beginner's Guide
The Beginner Witch's Collection Book Four
Poppets, Voodoo Dolls and Effigies
Creating Magic Entities:
Familiars, Thought Forms & Energy Balls
Spellcasting a beginner's guide
The 4 Pillars of Witchcraft
The Beginner Witch's Collection, Book Five
Cleansing, Charging & Consecrating
5 Tenets of Magic:
Purpose, Concentration, Regularity, Intent &
Focus
Scrying and Mirror Magic
~Magic~ Creation, Transformation &
Manifestation

Fiction Books by E.M. Fairchilde

The NEK Series
The Misfit Coven Series, TBA
The Water Street Witch
The Witch Next Door

Disclaimer

The methods described in this book are my personal thoughts and experiences. I realize others may practice the craft differently, and so, may use different methods. My methods are not intended to be a definitive set of instructions for using the craft. You may discover other methods and materials to carry out and achieve the same results. The craft is all about personal power, and using that special power to achieve, and manifest your life goals.

This book is not a life manual. The contents are not intended to offend. If you do not believe in the paranormal, then this book is not for you.

I hope my simplified approach to magic will help you.

Blessed be!

Forward

If you're reading this book, more than likely, you are interested in magic, the Wiccan way, or are beginning your journey. My hope is that the information provided will help. I believe, as I state throughout this book, that practicing magic is not complicated, it is an elemental down to earth, way of life. In a sense, we all use magic daily; we're just not aware of it.

We become aware of our power when we actively pursue the ins and outs of making things happen intentionally. If you do not believe in Wicca, Paganism, or Witchcraft, then this book is not for you.

Otherwise, for those of you who are interested in learning some of the many facets of Paganism, Wicca, or Witchcraft and want to try something different, welcome to my magical world! Use this book as general knowledge as you begin your journey.

I believe using magic should be simple. Don't get bogged down with the words used to define the process. They only feel intimidating to you now because they are not part of your current daily vocabulary. Once you know the basics of magic, and the definitions of words that will come up often in your quest for knowledge about magic, you'll be comfortable. I hope my simplified approach will help you, so if you want to learn a few things about the craft, feel free to use the information for a thought-provoking journey. Blessed be!

E. M. Fairchilde

Harm and Consequences

Everything we do in life has consequences. If you are not already practicing, weigh the consequences you think will occur as you journey through magic. And if practicing the craft will benefit you in a good way then go ahead and begin. Remember, like many words, the word consequences have both negative and positive meanings.

'Do no harm, harm no one, no harm be done' is an interesting concept. And it is an excellent concept to follow. But harm is a vague word and an even more nebulous idea. If I harm someone who has done harm to me, is this a bad idea? If a killer is harmed while being pursued, is pursuing him a bad idea? You will have to decide for yourself what harm means to you and then live with your decisions as to how you use it.

Consequence is another interesting word and an even more interesting concept.

Consequences can be positive or negative. But, sometimes, until all is said and done with certain actions, it is hard to know if the outcomes have been positive or negative.

Using magic opens the door to many would-be consequences so be sure you can live with the outcome of your work. Magic is like anything, how you use it is what determines its good or bad label. A knife can be good or bad, it depends on what you do with it. Magic is the same. It's an energy that you manipulate.

Practicing as a solitary witch leaves it entirely up to you the kinds of magic you work with. Some individuals, covens and groups frown on manipulative magic. You will have to decide for yourself your comfort level with the many facets of magic. If something doesn't resonate with you, don't do it, because the outcome may not be what you were expecting. On the other hand, if you are open to all or most kinds of magic because you are trying to find what *will* work for you, then use it. But, use it wisely.

One thing to consider when trying out new magical practices is the *way* you carry out your practice determines your outcome. For example, just as some types of magic may be more manipulative than others, so might lighter magic if you are using it in a manipulative manner.

If you create your own spells and magic tools, you will know precisely how and what they are used for and what they mean because you are the creator and your intentions are clear. However, if you purchase spells or tools, make sure you know what they mean, and how to use them because some spells and tools may have negative connotations based solely on the person's thought process who created them. This would come apparent to you if the spell or tools you purchased were supposed to render a positive result, but the opposite occurred.

Always cleanse anything new you've found or purchased whether it is for use with your practice or not because you have no idea how many hands and energies it had passed through before it became yours. You certainly don't want bad energy to permeate around and through you because it may hinder your life, livelihood, home, and practice. There are many simple cleansing tools and spells that don't involve an extensive ritual. Just like shielding, your shield can be as simple as saying, "shields up." Your cleansing can be just as simple. Find what works for you.

Energy

Energy is an interesting concept. Everything revolves around energy. When I worked for corporate America, I used to have a saying, "You put your energy into a project, and it works, you take your energy out of the project and it falls apart." And that was always true for me. But if that's true, then why is it that some people can accomplish what others can't? I believe it circles back to energy. If you are attempting something that is not for you, it won't work no matter what you put into it; in fact, you may just be wasting good energy that might be better used elsewhere.

All magic is manipulative because we use tools and energies to perform rituals for an outcome. Energy is neither good nor bad, just as manipulating energy is neither good nor bad, again it depends on how we manipulate it. For example, I can use my fire bowl as part of a ritual I am performing by burning a paper on which I've written something I wish to banish from my life. In this case, the fire (energy) is contained, and when the paper is burned, the fire goes out. But that same fire (energy) can also be destructive when it is not watched and gets out of control. So, we can say that energy can be constructive and or destructive. But even that is a vague statement because the fire we are using to burn the paper is destructive in that it destroys the paper. The only difference is that we control one fire. We manipulate the fire to do our will.

When it comes to magic, it is all about how we use energy, how we control it, how we move it around to accomplish what we set out to accomplish. So, when it comes to what some call manipulative magic, yes, it is manipulative, but it depends on how we manipulate it that makes it good or bad.

I know a person who doesn't practice the craft. At least she doesn't practice it consciously. Yet, whenever she really wants something, she energizes herself to such a high frequency that she obtains what she wants almost immediately.

She says she focuses on only what she wants and nothing else, and she manifests. Her energy is high. I've seen her do this repeatedly. But, here's the crux, because she doesn't think through what she's going after, in other words, she doesn't have a plan, a lot of the time she has wasted her energy because what she has gotten turns out not to be what she thought it was to begin with. She goes through an equal amount of energy getting rid of what she set out to get.

My own energy is scattered, and I must work hard to reign it in so I can use it for my magic. One reason I love practicing the craft is it forces me to focus on what I'm doing with my energy. I've used metaphysical concepts most of my life, so turning to the craft was easy. In a lot of ways, it's all remarkably similar. It's all about focused energy and how you manipulate that energy. So, reign in your energy, and focus, focus, focus! You *are* the creator!

Ceremonies and Mood

I love ceremonies, and for me, a ceremony is created by setting a mood.

I create a mood for almost everything I do. My mood enhancers are usually music and smell. I play smooth jazz, barely discernible when writing. If I am creating artistically, I play early rock and for rituals such as cleansing, charging, and consecrating, I play low, scarcely perceptible background sounds such as babbling brooks, wind, ocean waves, and birds.

I find my work more natural, more desirable, and more successful if I create an atmosphere. For sleep, I fill muslin bags with Lavender, Bay Leaf, Rosemary, and even Sage to slip in my pillowcase.

My morning ceremony for stretching is facing the north and stretching and saying, "Guide me today northern energy," facing the east, stretching and saying, "Guide me today eastern energy," facing the south, and stretching and saying, "Guide me today southern energy, and finally facing the west and stretching, and saying, "Guide me today western energy." This is a ceremony with a little bit of magic and some healthy stretching thrown in.

I burn candles and incense throughout the day because I love the smell, and I believe the fragrance keeps me and my home in a constant state of protection.

Does creating a mood and atmosphere take more time? Yes, but there are no short cuts if you desire success, and this is what works for me.

Focus on your intent: Focus keenly on what it is you want to accomplish for your spell, ritual, or ceremony. Visualize it working for you, your home, your workplace, or another person. Rid your mind of all unwanted or negative energies. See and feel the adverse and negative energy leave. Speak your incantation with conviction, strength, and force of will in the perfect atmosphere you've created.

The comfort and pleasure of your atmosphere, the endurance of your will, and the strength of your voice will bring forth your desired effect.

The ceremonies I use, I consider prep work for my magic. My ceremonies are nontraditional and fit my needs and comfort for practicing my kind of magic. But you are certainly welcome to use any of them if you feel the need to prep for your ceremonies. Since there is not a dogmatic approach to eclectic, solitary, chaos magic, you should perform it; however, you wish. Do what works for you!

Contents

Banish—eliminate
Bind—tie-up
Curse—cast evil, doom, or
misfortune on a person,
group, or action
Hex—bewitch, charm, or
jinx

Introduction

This is a beginner's guide written in simple terms to make it easy for you to harness and practice using your personal power to achieve personal goals. Sometimes we complicate things and make them more difficult than need be, and this causes confusion, so this book is written using simple and basic terms. The key to using your personal power is focus, repetition, and intent. Keep it simple and focus, don't get overwhelmed or bogged down with terminologies.

If what you do works for you, continue to do it. Call your craft whatever you want. Since using the elements to achieve your goals tends towards nature-based beliefs, it may fall within the realms of Paganism or Wicca. And, you may see yourself as a practitioner of witchcraft, using magic and divination. You may, in fact, call yourself a witch. I consider myself an Eclectic, Solitary, even Chaotic witch. I create my own methods, spells, chants, affirmations, incantations, and rituals. I don't necessarily turn away from traditional tried-and-true methods because I use the basics that people of the craft have used for centuries, but I use them my own way. Moon charts for spells, the elements, candles, herbs, spices, oils, and trinkets are all part of what makes me an Eclectic Witch.

Learning to use **banishing, binding, cursing, and hexing techniques** for divination ensures consistency of the practice. The more you learn, use, and apply the basics, the more accomplished you will become. And you will feel competent and secure in using your personal power to achieve your goals. And, by mastering the basics, you can move on quickly to more advanced practices.

I will be using the terms **banishing, binding, cursing, and hexing** frequently. Additionally, I have added more words to the glossary. Understanding the meaning of these words will help you on your journey of using banishing, binding, cursing, and hexing as part of your magic.

When using banishing, binding, cursing, or hexing, you are moving away from white magic and leaning towards black magic. Some covens, groups, and circles frown upon this kind of magic. If you are part of a coven, group, or circle, you might want to check with them to see where they stand with this type of magic. If you work as a solitary, it's your choice to banish, bind, curse, or hex. While I have no problem with these techniques, I would caution you to know the consequences of what you are attempting.

All of this is simple when you break it down. With all witchcraft practices, remember the most basic rule, **'do no harm, harm no one, no harm be done.'** You are responsible for what you send out to the universe.

Banishing

First and foremost, if you feel you need to attempt banishing, be absolutely sure of that need. Banishing can be permanent and at some point, in time, if you change your mind, it may be difficult to undo what you have done.

As stated in the glossary, banishing is the act of driving away negativity, evil, adverse conditions, even negative people. We use banishing spells to drive away anything we think of as a threat or a nuisance, be that a person, obstacle, debt, disease, or even negative habits such as smoking or drug usage.

Banishment magic is versatile and may be used for a variety of things. If you feel the need to banish, you should work with the different energies needed to accomplish the task at hand and then go with what you think is most comfortable to you. But you have to be careful and only have the highest of intentions when banishing.

In some circles, banishing is considered manipulative and not allowed. The idea that people do spells, incantations, and or rituals to bend the elements to their will does seem manipulative, especially when this is done *without* the knowledge of another. It is one thing to banish evil, negativity, or disease but is something entirely different when you banish people. Not so much from your life because some people, people who are no good for you probably need to be banished. But, banishing them to someplace negative, or to some negative position is perhaps not good for your karma. So, if you do attempt banishing people, always banish them to their highest good. This way if they end up in a negative place, it's obviously their highest good.

Even so, banishing is your choice; if you belong to a coven or group that frowns on banishing, but you still want to attempt it, you may want to reassess your membership.

For me personally, I have no objection using banishing if it is used right and for the highest good.

Sometimes we are faced with situations and people that are not right for us, and we need to get away from the negativity. And if nothing else has worked to end the dire situation, then banishing is one way of accomplishing that feat.

Keywords associated with Banishing—

Manipulative magic
Highest good
Free will
The elements (fire, earth, water, air)
Taglock
Reflective
Drive away
Eliminate
Dismiss
Mirror
The elements

Ceremonies and rituals: There are many avenues to banishing. You can freeze banish, poppet banish, fire banish, balloon banish, burial banish, and or paper banish (write it, cut it) are all ways to achieve your goal.

All of the ways I listed require either a picture or a written description of the person you want to remove from your life. This also applies to circumstances. A taglock (see taglock in the glossary provided below) is desirable, but not always necessary.

If you are attempting to banish a behavior or condition that affects you, you can always use a mirror and reflect the behavior away from you and back to wherever it belongs. *I have a specific mirror I use for this purpose. It is a double-sided tortoiseshell mirror that opens like a book.

If you want to try fire, you can use a picture and write on the back of the image that this person is released from your life to their highest good and their hold on you is discharged. It's best to use a black candle for this fire ceremony as black is associated with banishing. As the picture burns, talk to the person as if they are in your presence and let them know you are using fire to burn off their presence in your life. This works best outdoors using your burning bowl. When the picture is burned, you can either bury the ashes or release them into the air.

I use a lot of fire ceremonies, this seems to work for me, and it is something I am comfortable doing. I also prefer to release the ashes into the air and not bury them.

Poppets and balloons can be used for banishing as well and are quite useful. You can make a poppet and release it by burning, drowning, freezing, or burying once you have completed your spell.

Balloons can have a picture of a person, or something written out about a specific condition or action tied to a string attached and released into the U.

Water can be useful as well. For example, if you have access to a river, stream, or even an ocean, you can do a water banishing. You can float that person or annoying activity or condition down-stream or out to sea, or you can even sink it. Sinking involves attaching your writing to a rock and dropping it as you speak your banishing words. And, you can also place your written material in a bottle and throw it out on the water as you speak your banishing words.

You can create or purchase a poppet and sew into the poppet whatever or whoever you want to banish and burn or bury the poppet. I create my own poppets because while I am in the creation process, I am visualizing what I want the poppet to achieve for me. Balloons are obvious, write your banishing ceremony down, attach it to a balloon and set it free. You can even write out your words *on* the balloon.

The opportunities for banishing using the elements (air, earth, wind, and fire) are endless!

Spells or incantations: Below are banish chants I use. You can see they are in no way manipulative. They are merely removing someone or something from my life. They are simple yet effective. You could use these with any of the ceremonies listed above, or you can use these as ideas to write your own incantations.

I banish _____ *(name of person)*

You brought discord into my life
And caused me turmoil and pain
My life holds no place for you
You will never affect me again.
Blessed be

I banish _____ *(a condition or situation)*
My life has no room for you
Release your hold on me
Move on, be gone, withdraw, depart
As I begin anew and restart.

Notes: Use these pages to write your own spells, rituals, and ideas.

_____
_____
_____
_____
_____
_____
_____
_____
_____
_____
_____
_____
_____
_____
_____
_____
_____
_____
_____

Binding

Binding is somewhat different from banishing. When using binding against another person, you are, in effect restricting them from attacking you in whatever form the attacks are taking place. For example, a person could be lying, cheating, or stealing from you, or you may be physically or mentally abused by the person. There is a multitude of reasons to bind another person. By binding, you are restricting your attacker by restraining them.

You could also bind a place, a behavior, or a condition. For example, you could bind yourself to a site you love, or a job you love.

And finally, you could bind yourself to a condition that you are hoping to achieve.

Some believe this is manipulative magic. Like banishing, I have no problem with binding if it is done for the right reasons and under the right circumstances.

Like all ritual work, binding can be light or dark, positive, or negative. As with all spell work, remember **'do no harm, harm no one, no harm be done.'**

On the light side, binding can be done to bring something into your life that you desire. In doing so, ensure your desire does not belong to another. You should not take something or someone that is not available or belongs to another.

The darker side of binding is getting rid of someone or something or gaining something out of spite or jealousy. Binding becomes manipulative spell work when you go after something or someone that belongs to another.

If you have tried everything else and have had no luck, then binding may be what you need to try. So, regardless of what you've read about binding, like all spell work, your intention and energy are what matters because binding is all about restricting and restraint. Your goal with binding is to restrict someone or something from causing havoc in your life, but the other side of binding is the desire to bind something to you or to bind yourself to something. You may love your job and bind yourself to it to ward away any negative energy from someone you work with. You may also like your house, and so you might bind yourself to it. You could bind a favored piece of jewelry to you so that you don't lose or misplace it.

Keywords associated with Binding—

Manipulative magic
Prevention
Handfasting
Restriction
Restraint
Personal protection
Taglock
Retaining
Confining
Knotting
The elements

Ceremonies and rituals: Things you might need to work on binding, poppet (represents a person), candles (assorted colors), paper, tablet, wood to write on or burn.

For binding rituals, you can use the same ceremonies as banishing. The difference is in the actual binding. When you bind, you will be using string, rope, or something that appeals to you to tie the paper, poppet, or whatever you use tightly.

A water ritual might go like this. If you need to stop a person from causing harm or chaos, you can do a couple of different things. You can get something that belongs to them, or you can use a picture, or if neither of those choices is possible, you can write it out using the person's name. So, let's say you can get something that belongs to the person. You will use ribbon, rope, or twine to start wrapping it around the item. As you wrap it tightly, you will need to say something about why you are doing this. You might say, "I bind you from all the chaos you are causing to me." You keep repeating the words until you have used all the binding material. At this time, you toss the item you

17

have bound into the water so that it will float away, or if you prefer, you can attach it to a heavy rock and let it sink to the bottom of the river, stream, lake, or ocean. As you are doing this, you imagine the person gone. You walk away and don't look back. It's over.

Spells or incantations: Where I place a blank line in an incantation, you can place a name, condition, or object if you want to use this as an incantation. These incantations are used as you bind your target.

I bind _____ (insert name)
You will never cross my path again
Or cause me hurt and pain
I bind you left, I bind you right,
You're gone forevermore.
Blessed be

I bind _____ (a condition or situation)
I bind you today, I bind you tonight
I bind you left; I bind you right.
I bind you tight, no more to be,
I bind you gone away from me.

Blessed be.

I bind _____ *(behavior)*
I bind your conduct,
It stops today
Hear me, don't test me
Or I'll send you away.
Blessed be.

Notes: Use these pages to write your own
spells, rituals, and ideas.

_____
_____
_____
_____
_____
_____
_____
_____
_____
_____
_____
_____
_____
_____
_____
_____
_____
_____
_____
_____
_____

Cursing

Cursing is used to stop, possibly harm, hold, or block a person. So, before you get into cursing, you might want to know all the ins and outs of what it is, what it isn't, and what to expect. Cursing is manipulative magic because the person or situation you are cursing isn't aware and has more than likely has not given you permission to curse him.

Cursing is generally negative and requires the use of negative energy to be performed correctly. When cursing, you have a select person, condition, or behavior in mind, it is not a generality. And you must be seriously finished with whatever is causing you pain. Curses are hard to undo once they're set in motion. So, be absolutely sure when you decide to curse, and then think about it for a little bit longer.

To explain cursing, I have a real-life story of what happened to me when I used cursing. It's called **No More Music**. I used to live in a condo. I was in a middle unit so there was someone on each side of me, above me, and another condo that backed up to mine.

I never heard a noise of any kind except for the condo to the left of me. The music they played was so loud, I could hear it through my bedroom and living room and into my office, which was at the opposite end of the condo. You can imagine how loud this music must have been if it could be heard through three sets of walls.

I tried to ignore it because it happened mainly on weekends, so it didn't disturb my work week. But one weekend, I'd had enough when the music started early in the day and continued into the night. It was also the day I was doing some marketing for my nine to five job for the following week. I couldn't concentrate.

I'd just returned from a trip to New Orleans, where I happened to stop in at a very famous voodoo shop. I'd purchased three voodoo dolls because they fascinated me. I wasn't practicing the craft at that time, as I said, the dolls merely fascinated me. When I unpacked from the trip, I set the dolls on my desk in the office at my condo.

The music from the condo next door had angered me, and my energy was almost raging. I grabbed one of the dolls, pulled out the pin, and stabbed the doll hard as I yelled NO MORE MUSIC, I CURSE YOU, NO MORE MUSIC.

The music didn't stop immediately, but it did stop. A couple of weeks later, the people were carrying boxes out of the condo and loading them into a moving truck. I stopped and asked them if they were moving, and the man said, "Our Jeep was broken into, this is not the place we want to live."

I didn't overthink it until I got inside, settled down, and saw the dolls on my desk. My shock was real. Did I cause that chain of events when I cursed them and their music? Energy is real! I didn't want their Jeep to be broken into, I wanted them to keep their music at a tolerable range. But I guess my emotion got in the way when I stabbed that doll.

To be honest, I wasn't sad about them moving because they were very inconsiderate and disturbing people with their music. When you live in an apartment or condo, you should be considerate towards your neighbors. I'd like to say that when the next family moved in that condo, they were quiet, but that wasn't the case. Finally, I decided condo living wasn't for me and I bought a house.

Keywords associated with Cursing—

Self-defense
Protection
Suggestion
Negative energy
Moving energy
Manipulating energy
Manipulative magic
Baneful magic
The Law of Return

Ceremonies and rituals: Some ways to curse another is to use their DNA, a picture, something written, create a poppet, leave something at the person's home, or in their car (that you've cursed).

Cursing generally involves heightened energy. So, it takes a little longer than other spells. You have to build your energy to make the curse effective. And usually, that energy is built on anger, or you are just plain fed up and there is no other way to work out the problem that is disrupting your life.

Spells or incantations:

I curse you _____ *(name or condition)*

I curse you here, I curse you now
I curse you forevermore
Stay away from me and mine
For I now close that door.
Blessed be

Notes: Use these pages to write your own spells, rituals, and ideas.

_____

_____

_____

_____

_____

_____

_____

_____

_____

_____

_____

_____

_____

_____

_____

_____

_____

_____

_____

_____

Hexing

In short, a hex is a spell or a charm. I use the word charm, not as a physical charm like a piece of jewelry but actually charming the target of your hex. Hexing is manipulative magic because the person you are hexing usually isn't aware and has more than likely not given you permission to hex him.

The goal of hexing is to make the target of the hex feel the same way you feel because of their actions against you. Hexing is a solution to a problem. Generally, hexing is a last resort but if you want to get something over with and nothing else you've tried works, go ahead and start hexing.

Hexing is not as simple as using a spell. Hexing requires a lot of energy; in fact, when you get to the point that you are going to hex, you are probably seriously fed up with whatever is bothering you and you've tried everything you can think of, and nothing has worked. Hexing generally involves heightened energy. So, it takes a little longer than other spells. You have to build your energy to make the hex effective.

To accomplish hexing, you should be fully aware and at peace with what you are doing because there is generally no taking back a hex.

When hexing, please understand there is an enormous difference in a life lesson and a deliberate act. For example, a person who sets out to do harm to you or your family is not a life lesson, it is an intentional act. However, if you keep doing something over and over and get the same negative result, you might want to look at what it is you are doing that keeps you reaping the same results. That is a life lesson.

You have to take stock and find out who you are and accept responsibility for your life. I say this because usually when a problem occurs, there are more than one side to the story. A favorite saying of mine is; there's this side of the story, and that side of the story, and the truth usually lies down the middle. How does this fit into hexing? Make sure you are hexing for the right reasons, and not for spite.

Keywords associated with Hexing—

Charm
Target
Manipulative magic
Accountability
Energy
Power
Force
Push
Dissolve

Ceremonies and rituals: So, let's say you are going to attempt a paper hex. You will write out everything your target has done to you.

The deeper you go emotionally to get to the truth is best. You need to put your energy into this, and it should put you in a state of anger with your target. This is the power behind the hex.

When you have finished writing and are in a powerful state, burn the paper. Instead of releasing or burying the ashes on the spot, you will take the ashes to a place of your choice, water, or maybe a field and then release them.

The idea for traveling is to release them away from your residence where you live. What you are doing is releasing how you feel about the target, the anger and hurt caused by him, her, or the condition. The idea is to send what you wrote back to whoever or whatever generated the state you are in. You will need a releasing incantation. Once you finish this, you cannot backtrack. Whatever or whoever you have hexed is finished, and you should consider it over.

Spells or incantations:

I hex _____ *(fill in the person or condition)*

I cast this hex upon you
You shall endure all that you have placed on me

33

I cast this hex upon you
You shall never more be free.
Blessed be.

I hex you _____ (name or condition)

May you forever suffer what you brought upon me
May you never know how my pain felt
May all your days be burdened
With what you have dealt.

Notes: Use these pages to write your own spells, rituals, and ideas.

_____

_____

_____

_____

_____

_____

_____

_____

_____

_____

_____

_____

_____

_____

_____

_____

_____

_____

_____

_____

_____

_____

_____

Care and Caution

Banishing, binding, cursing, and hexing have their place in magical practices. Use your gut feeling and common sense when choosing to use any or all of these actions. You certainly don't want bad energy, people, or situations to permeate around and through you because it may hinder your life, livelihood, home, and practice.

If you include a chant while you banish, bind, curse, or hex, remember the strength and power of your convictions and voice are critical in accomplishing your desired effect. Weak convictions and voices may hinder your work.

You must have faith in yourself and feel it and believe it!

Since banishing, binding, cursing, and hexing tend to fall into gray and black magic, here is an excerpt from my book *The Colors of Magic*, you might want to check it out if you decide to work with manipulative magic.

White Magic is generally done with good intent for the practitioner and the receiver if you are doing it upon request for another. In other words, the receiver grants permission.

Grey Magic is generally done with good intent and for help, but the receiver may not be aware the practitioner is doing magic for them. Permission may not necessarily be granted by the receiver.

Black Magic is supposedly done against the receiver and without his knowledge. Generally, it is said that black magic is done to harm and is for selfish purposes. I personally disagree with both those statements.

Permission, understanding, and intent are key words when using magic. The intention is powerful because if your intent is not strong, your magic will not be reliable.

Your intent must be spot on for magic to work. I believe most people who use, and practice magic fully understand the outcomes and consequences. However, with black magic, the receiver may not understand what is happening to him. Here again, under certain circumstances, I have no problem with this because there is no help for some people and in those cases, you must do what you must do. So long as you protect yourself and understand there may be consequences.

Practice, practice, practice! And, log your journey. When you find your niche, you will know you are home.

Finally, should you become adept at **banishing, binding, cursing, and hexing,** use the practices wisely and sparingly, and as a final effort to end bad situations.

Tools of the Trade

Banishing, binding, cursing, and hexing spell work can be slightly different from other spell work because you may travel away from your circle to accomplish the spell.

For example, you may start your spell by creating a poppet, or a tablet, or something in writing at your usual place of practice but you may dispose of the completed spell in a location where there is a large body of water, a cliff, or even an open field. If you do travel to an area such as the ones I mentioned, you should still follow the basic practices of drawing a circle where you stand and cleansing the area of negativity as much as possible.

The following list is filled with items you may wish to use when doing manipulative magic.

Pepper, the hotter, the better is used in making pepper powder which can be used for banishing.

Garlic and arrowroot are used when hexing. If your hex is written, you can charge the paper with these two products.

Binding requires some type of rope, string, wire, or ribbon to tie up the target or condition. To make a statement, tying up your chosen talisman with a black ribbon is quite useful.

You can also use ice to freeze your target. Using ice requires you to write out what you are trying to accomplish, place it in a jar half-filled with water, add to it whatever you think will help the spell work succeed, do your incantation and then freeze it. After a while, when you feel you have accomplished your goal, you can release the target to the forces that be by getting rid of the ice.

If you are going to use candles for banishing, binding, cursing, or hexing, you should use black. You can use whatever size candle you want. Believe it or not, I use birthday candles for the majority of my spell work. I only use larger candles if I feel a spell calls for the candle to burn for a longer length of time.

When creating oils for charging, I start out with olive oil as the carrier. A good banishing oil I use is made with the following essential oils, pine, peppermint, pepper oil, and rue oil. I don't make large batches so my concoctions will only be maybe an eighth cup of the carrier oil and then a drop or two of the essential oils. You can add crushed red pepper to the oil or make pepper powder to use with the oil. Pepper powder is made with red pepper, cayenne pepper, and black pepper. Grind the peppers until they are fine and add to baking soda or arrowroot powder.

Herbs that are beneficial in the oils and powders used for banishing, binding, cursing, and hexing are most kinds of pepper, ginger, mustard seed, poppy seed, and cacti. Then there are the poisonous herbs such as nightshade, hemlock, and henbane. Later I will be doing a beginner's guide on oils, herbs, and stones used for magic.

Finally, I have a supply of little brown bottles like the ones in the picture above that I use for my oils and powders. Be sure and label any concoctions you use in your magic. And I encourage you to make your own oils and powders instead of buying them.

Glossary

I want to familiarize you with some words that may be intimidating for beginners regarding the study and use of Wicca, Paganism, and magic. Some people may disagree with these very basic definitions of words associated with magic, but I keep things simple. Throughout this book, words, and phrases I feel are important are bolded, so pay special attention to those words and phrases. If anything piques your interest, feel free to do more thorough research. I have learned to take things in stride and use what works for me to keep life less complicated. There are, of course, many more words and terms associated with the craft. The words in this glossary are for beginners.

Abracadabra: A mystic word used when doing incantations, spells, or even during rituals. Typically, this word is used by magicians when performing magic tricks on stage. Also, it was used in olden times to ward off illness, misfortune, and or harm. *Some may say this has no place when practicing the craft; however, it can, especially if it has meaning to you. I use the word with intensity when I point two fingers, my middle and pointer finger at someone or something as I say words like ENOUGH!

Altar: An altar is your sacred space. You decide where your altar is located and what goes on it. Generally, whatever you feel connected to, or whatever tools move you, is what should go on your altar. An altar is very personal.

Alexandrian Witch: An Alexandrian Witch is part of a movement founded in the 1960s called Alexandrian Wicca. This movement is connected to Gardnerian Wicca but uses Qabalah and ceremonial magic as well.

Amulet: An object that is used to attract luck or positive energy. It can be worn or placed on your altar or any location where it may be needed.

Anointing Oil: Oil that has been charged (see charging) and blessed. Anointing oil can be made from a variety of oils, depending on the spell work being done. It is considered sacred.

Anointing oil is consecrated oil and is used for specific purposes depending on the oil. For example, oil for charging candles for a prosperity spell is cinnamon, myrrh and frankincense.

Augury Witch: A witch who works between cosmic forces and a person on a spiritual quest.

Banish: When you banish something or someone, you send it away.

Banishing: The act of driving away negativity, evil, negative conditions, even negative people. Banishing spells are used to drive away anything you think of as a threat or a nuisance be that a person, obstacle, debt, disease, or even negative habits such as smoking, alcohol, or drug use.

Beltane: The Sabbat celebrated on the first day of May.

Besom: The besom is a broom you use to sweep away negative energy. I have two Besoms; one is sprinkled with cinnamon, which is a powerful spice used in many potions. By sweeping away negative energy, you are, in effect blessing and protecting the space you have swept. You should always sweep your circle before you do spell work.

Binding: The act of restricting actions, binding can be positive or negative. You can bind something to you or bind it so that it cannot come near you. Binding can be used with people, objects, places, or even situations. For example, you can bind yourself to your job so that you cannot lose it. Binding is about restricting, controlling, and stopping certain things from happening.

Black Magic: Black magic is usually considered magic that is used to draw evil spirits to do your bidding.

Black Moon: The black moon is the dark moon.

Blood Moon: October full moon.

Blue Moon: Generally, a blue moon is an extra full moon occurring over the period of a month. It is an extra full moon.

Book of Shadows: A BOS is a book of your own creation. It is used to transcribe your work such as spells, rituals, and what worked as well as what didn't work. It is something you create. It is your Wiccan journal.

Casting a Circle: You cast a circle when doing spell work. The circle is your sacred space. It is swept with your Besom and can be charged with anointing oil. Use whatever oil goes with the spell work you are attempting. The circle is filled with the energy you put into it with your intent. So, give it your all. The more you energize your circle the more powerful your spell work will be.

*I use chalk for drawing my circle. You can purchase a big tub of large sticks of colored chalk and use them for this purpose.

Cauldron: A cauldron can be as simple as a bowl. It does not have to be a huge black pot set up on a tripod and bubbling over a fire. But, if you want to use a black cast-iron pot and place it on a tripod, then by all means do so. If something you already possess moves you to use it as a cauldron, then bless it, charge it, and use it. Find a bowl that feels right to you. I have a copper bowl set aside for that purpose.

Centering: Centering is achieved by meditating before a ritual is performed. It is essential to be centered and focused before beginning any magic work.

Ceremonial Witch: A Ceremonial Witch practices ceremonies and rituals by the book.

Ceremony: A ceremony can be considered a religious, sacred, or a formal event. Rituals and spell work can be ceremonial. By making your spell work ceremonial you are adding more intent.

Chalice: A chalice is one of many tools used during spell work. It can be a talisman, it can be used on your altar, or it can be used as an amulet.

Chant: Chanting can be used to charge your spells. By chanting a spell your mind goes into a meditative state. Your spell become melodious and you tend to concentrate on the spell leaving the outside world behind. This adds intent to your spell.

Chaos Magic: In my opinion, Chaos Magic and Eclectic Witchery go hand in hand. Using chaos magic, you are merely taking from different types of magic and using the approach that works for you. In Chaos Magic, it is your belief in what you are doing that achieves the results, not the ceremony leading up to it.

Charge: Charge a talisman using the sun, moon, salt, or a ritual as simple as passing the talisman through a candle flame. You may charge an item by chanting, meditating, or dancing. Purified water may also be used to charge your talisman. Remember to create a ritual by saying something like by my power you are charged and empowered to work for me, so it must be. When you charge an item, you are energizing it for a specific purpose.

Charm: A charm is both physical and mental. Physically it is a talisman or amulet and is worn as jewelry or is used to create tools of the trade. Mentally charm is focusing the mind to obtain a desired outcome. Both types of charm can be used in casting spells and doing rituals. Wiccans use charms to attract or repel certain energies to bring about a desired changes and outcomes.

Chaste Moon: March full moon.

Circle: A Circle is a group of people that come together to perform magic. Or, it can be a sacred space you create to do your own magic. *Again, I create my own circles with colored chalk.

Cleanse: When you cleanse an object, you are preparing it to use in your spell work. Cleansing rids the object of all negativity. Cleansing may also be done to your circle, altar, and sacred space. It goes without saying you want to cleanse yourself as well to send any negative energy on its way before you perform your magic. You may also use a sage cleanse by passing an object through sage smoke, or dancing around your circle or sacred space with the sage.

*Cinnamon is a great spice to use for cleansing.

Cold Moon: December full moon.

Corn Moon: August full moon, also known as the Green Plant full moon.

Coven: A coven is a gathering or community of witches. A high Priest and Priestess usually rule over a coven, and there are usually thirteen members, but there can be more Coven members gather to train, to perform rituals, and celebrate Sabbats. You must be initiated into a coven.

*I am not part of a coven.

Crystal Witch: Crystal Witches work with crystals and stones for healing and balancing. They generally have extensive knowledge about stones, rocks, and crystals.

Curse: A curse is performed for reasons such as retaliation, and is usually negative, or fueled by negative energy. Sometimes a person is cursed by another out of jealousy. If you are considering performing a curse, remember the law of do no harm, harm no one, no harm be done because curses can come back to you.

Cursing: Performing a curse, thought to be manipulative magic.

Dark Moon: The dark moon phase occurs when the moon cannot be seen due to the way it is situated in relation to the Earth.

Dianic Witch: A Dianic Witch practices by calling on the Goddess Diana. They pay homage to all of Diana's aspects, maiden, mother, and crone.

Divination: Divination is the act of foretelling the future, or to gain insight about a situation.

Dowsing: When dowsing, you are doing a type of divination to locate specific objects. Generally, some type of divining rod is used when dowsing.

Draconian Witch: Draconian Witches practice dragon magic.

Draw: When drawing in magic, the witch is attempting to draw a certain kind of energy to the person or situation. A drawing spell is used to bring energy to the practitioner. You may want to draw abundance, love, or health to yourself or someone or something.

Dream Journal: A dream journal is simply a journal you keep near your bed in order to transcribe your dreams upon awakening when they are still fresh on your mind. Dreams can be recurrent. They can give you messages, warnings, or needed information. Some people use dream pillows that contain herbs that enhance dreams. Dream work is important because dreams can provide needed information to your waking life.

*My dreams are vivid, so I keep a journal and pen beside my bed.

Dress: By dressing an object in spell work, you are preparing it for use with your ritual. You may use sage smoke, oils, or trinkets, or all three. With oils, you prepare the oil for the spell, and rub the candle with the oil. When dressing a candle, you are imprinting your intention upon the candle.

Dressing Oil: Dressing oil is a specially prepared oil applied to spell and ritual objects before using them to sanctify, charge and prepare them for use or after assembling them to charge and activate them. This is called "dressing" or "fixing" the object.

Druid: Druidic Witches focus on Mother Earth in their practice. They do their work in wooded parks and forests. They are nature based. They are in touch with super-natural spirits as part of their craft.

Eclectic Witch: Eclectic witches do not follow any certain religion or practice. Generally, they are intuitive and work from there. They have studied many schools-of-thought and work from all of them.

Effigy: An effigy is an image created or bought that is not drawn. It is an image that is used to resemble a person or an entity. A voodoo doll is an example of an effigy. It is used in spell work and is generally destroyed after it is used.

Elemental Witch: An Elemental Witch is a witch who primarily works with the elements.

Energy Ball: An Energy Ball is a ball of energy formed by you and sent out to the universe to do your bidding.

Energy Work: Energy work is done to change the energy in the energy field. For example, we do energy work to get rid of negativity. When sweeping or circle we are doing energy work. Chanting and meditating also is a form of energy work.

Equinox: The equinox occurs twice a year. There is an autumnal and vernal equinox. During an equinox daylight and darkness are even.

Esbat: Esbats are times of spiritual gatherings for a coven. Spell work, and or worship take place when the coven gathers together. This usually happens on a full moon.

Essence: The essence of something is the truest nature of that thing, the essence defines the quality of a thing and determines the character of it.

Essential Oil: Essential oils are fragrant oils that come from plants and are used in spell work.
*I keep the main essential oils on hand for charging.

Evil: Evil is a dark concept that is generally thought to be a force of darkness and destruction.

Evil Eye: The evil eye is a look that is given to project a curse, or a feeling of disruption. It is done by staring at a person and sending vibes. You can also create or purchase an evil eye to repel negative energy.

Evocation: Invoking a spirit or a deity. Calling it into spell work, bringing it to the forefront.

Exorcism: An exorcism takes place when an evil entity or negative energy needs to be expelled from a person or a place.

Faerie Witch: Faerie Witches seek information from faery folk and nature spirits as part of their practice.

Familiar: A familiar is a helper, a servant used in spell work or magic. It is generally in the form of an animal. Familiars are bonded to the person they serve, but they tend to have their own personalities. For example, my familiar is my cat named Lola. She came to me through some rather strange circumstances.

*Lola's picture is on my author profile page at the beginning of this book.

Fire Bowl: A fire bowl is used for containing a fire. It is generally propped up on a stand and is used during spell work. Fire bowls can be used indoors (if they are small) or outdoors. Fire bowls are good for burning effigies or lists once a spell is complete.

Full Moon: The moon phase where the entire moon is illuminated and can be seen. This usually occurs once per month.

Forces of nature: Air, earth, water, and fire are the forces of nature invoked in spell work. Each force is used for a different reason and is associated with a different condition. The forces of nature are also part of the pentagram and or pentacle.

Gaggle of Witches: A gaggle is a group of witches that lacks organization.

Gardnerian Witch: Generally, these witches follow Gerald Gardner's kind of Wicca that emerged in the 1950's. Gerald Gardner is known as the father of Wicca. Gardnerian Witches must be initiated before they can become true Gardnerian Witches.

Gray Witch: Gray witches practice a balanced kind of witchcraft, between white and black magic.

Green Witch: A Green Witch practices by communicating with Mother Earth. She uses tools made from natural materials. She focuses on nature.

Grimoire: You have probably seen and or heard the word Grimoire. In movies, it is a book that appears to be magical and mystical, and even somewhat secretive. A Grimoire is a book akin to a textbook that contains information about magic, spells, potions, rituals, and well you get the idea. The difference between a Grimoire and a Book of Shadows is the Grimoire is the work of one or many persons who authored it, and a Book of Shadows is your own creation. You may certainly use a Grimoire for information, and there are many out there, just as there are many websites where you may find information.

Grounding: Grounding is the process of connecting with and becoming aware of our physical body and how it is connected to the Earth. It allows us to drain negative energy into the Earth as we draw good energy back to us. Grounding helps you to equalize your energy so you can focus while doing your spiritual work. Grounding allows us to eliminate excess energy.

Handfasting: Handfasting is a magic ritual that binds two people together for a specific time frame.

Hare Moon: May moon.

Harvest Moon: The harvest moon is a full moon that occurs at the autumnal equinox.

Hay Moon: July full moon, also known as the Mead moon.

Hearth Witch: Similar to a Kitchen Witch.

Hedge Witch: A Hedge Witch travels between worlds. She communicates with the spiritual realm delivering messages between worlds.

Herbs: Herbs are woody plants that flower and are used in spell work.

Hereditary Witch: A Hereditary Witch is born into the practice. Her family members have passed down their craft from generation to generation.

Hex: A hex is a curse that is put on a person or a place. It is spell work that can be negative.

Hexing: Performing a hex.

Imbolc: The Sabbat celebrated around the second day of February.

Incantation: A group of words created to cast a spell. Though not connected to any specific religion, incantations are used in many religions. Incantations are often thought of as being enchanting because they are used to create a desired effect. They can be spoken or sung. They can be intoxicating and put the person reciting the incantation in a spell-like state.

Incense: Incense is a fragrant material that produces smoke and is used in spell work. It can be used by itself or with herbs and oils.

Initiation: Initiation is the ceremony when a person is admitted to a coven. It is not necessary to join a coven. But if you choose to do so you will go through an initiation ceremony.

Intent: Intent is the basis of magical spell work. Intent is resolve and determination. The stronger the intent, the better your chance for success when doing spell work. Intent is serious eager attention you put into your spell work.

Invoke: Invoking is to summon, bring forth, or draw a spirit or deity you can communicate with.

Karma: The belief that what you do, your thoughts, your actions come back to you.

Karma can be good or bad. It is part of your spiritual path.

Kitchen Witch: A Kitchen Witch uses practicality in her craft. She works with recipes and potions. Her home is her sacred place.

Lammas: The harvest Sabbat celebrated in August.

Litha: The Sabbat celebrated as the summer solstice around June twenty-first.

Lunar Day: Lunar day begins when the moon rises and ends when the moon sets. Knowing when this occurs can benefit spell work.

Lunar Eclipse: A lunar eclipse occurs during a full moon. The sun, earth, and moon are in alignment. occurs when the Sun, Earth and Moon are in syzygy or perfect (or near perfect) alignment. Lunar eclipse spell work is powerful.

Lunar Witch: A lunar Witch follows lunar cycles as she practices her rituals.

Mabon: The Sabbat celebrated as the Autumn Equinox around September twenty-first.

Magic: Magic is neither religious nor scientific. Throughout history magic has conjured up negative and positive connotations, depending on the century, and the ideology of the faction in charge. Magic is the use of personal power to bring about change, to the physical world. Magic is brought forth by a person's will, his belief in his power. Wicca and magic go hand in hand. Wiccans use magic. While some believe magic is evil, paranormal, or super-natural, people who use magic believe it is available to anyone who believes in the power of his own mind. There is nothing abnormal about it, it is merely using and channeling personal power with or without the use of aids or tools. It is a natural force. You can't see it, you can't touch it, but once you get good at it, you can feel it when it's working! Believe in magic, or don't believe in it, either way for you personally you're right.

Magical Petitions: Magical petitions are simply written spell work. Generally, the desire is written on some type of paper, sealed, and after the spell is activated, it is released by fire in a burning bowl, or buried. It can also be saved in your BOS (Book of Shadows). It can be a single spell or part of a bigger spell that has many parts. I generally write my desires, meditate over them, then burn them and release the ashes outdoors to the U. I find that writing my desires makes me concentrate more deeply and my intent becomes stronger.

Magick: The same as magic defined below. However, the spelling was changed so people wouldn't confuse stage magic by magicians with practitioners of paranormal magic associated with Pagan type religions.

Manipulative magic: Magic that is done against a person without their permission, because it may impact their free will.

Meditation: A process of turning inward, quieting the mind, and reflecting. Meditation is a time you set aside to gather yourself, to renew and recharge yourself.

Mojo Bag: A mojo bag is a small bag containing magical items that are charged and used during spell work. The bag contains specific items depending on the spells. A witch can have more than one mojo bag.

Necromancy: Necromancy is used in spell work to contact and communicate with the dead. It is believed the dead can provide insights into situations that the living cannot see, such as foretelling future events.

New Moon: The new moon is the moon phase that usually cannot be seen from Earth or appears as a slight slender crescent. See dark moon.

Nocturnal Witch: A Nocturnal Witch works at night and draws her powers from the darkness.

Occult: Simply put, the occult is the study of paranormal, metaphysical, mystical, magical, and or super-natural events. The very word occult tends to take on an evil or negative feeling. There is nothing evil about study the occult.

Omen: An omen is a sign of something to come, an event that may be positive or negative. In your study of Wicca, you may get 'feelings' of something that is about to happen. Or, you may have dreams about something that is about to happen. Your omens are your omens. Omens have different meanings for different people. If an event occurs every time you see or find something—that may be an omen. It could be something as simple as finding a feather.

Ostara: The Sabbat celebrated as the Spring Equinox on March twenty-first.

Out of Body Experience: An OBE is an out-of-body experience. It simply means your soul travels outside your body. This frequently happens when a person is sleeping, or in a dream state. People have reported out-of-body experiences when in an accident, undergoing surgery, or in a dangerous situation. An out-of-body experience can be intentional (through meditation) or accidental (such as leaving the body during a traumatic experience).

Pagan: Pagan covers a lot of different faiths, usually earth based. Pagans follow a spiritual path centered in nature. Most Pagans are polytheistic. That is, they believe in many deities.

Pair Moon: June full moon.

Pendulum: A pendulum is an object attached to yarn, string, chain, or even wire. It can be any type of object, but should be something that you relate to, something that you connect with on a deeper level. It is used for both dowsing and divining. To use the pendulum, you hold it over something and concentrate. The pendulum swings in a certain direction which will then give you the answer to your question. For example, a pendulum held over a pregnant woman's body that swings a certain way can predict the sex of the baby. But the pendulum has no power of its own, the answer is coming from the subconscious of the person holding the pendulum. You have the power, and the answer is coming through you.

Pentacle: A pentacle is a five-pointed star, the points represent spirit, earth, air, water, and fire. It is encased in a circle. The pentacle is used in magic for spell-work. It can also be made into jewelry and worn.

Pentagram: The pentagram is also called a pentacle, and like the pentacle is a religious symbol for Pagans. The star has five points, the top point of the pentagram represents Spirit, this is where all the elements come together. The upper right is water, the upper left is air, the lower right is fire, and the lower left is earth. The pentagram like the pentacle is used for spell-work. It can be placed on your altar, or it can be your altar if you do not have a dedicated altar. You of course have to charge your pentagram with your energy when doing spell work. You can also buy jewelry in the shape of a pentagram and wear it for whatever purpose you decide.

Personal Power: Personal power is the power that emanates through you to perform your magic.

Poppet: Poppets and voodoo dolls are used interchangeably. The dolls are made in the image of the individual of the spell you are creating. If you make your own poppet, you can use it for love, prosperity, to overcome illness, protection, banishing, or binding. Once the poppet has been used, and the spell has been accomplished, the doll should be disposed of properly. A poppet can be an amulet, or a talisman. The dolls can be made from several different materials. I use sticks, moss, and material to create my dolls. I use a variety of trinkets to make my dolls specific for the purpose it represents.

Pow-Wow Witch: Pow-Wow witches are rooted in Pennsylvania and practice a type of Germanic witchcraft that is over 400 years old. They focus on healing rituals and spells.

Purification: Purification ceremonies are performed to clear away negativity, undesired influences, bad energy, or anything that invades you or your space. People who practice the craft use purification ceremonies to clear the way for their ceremonies or rituals. They not only clean their workspace, they also purify themselves, and their tools, such as wands, pendulums, candles, bowls, and anything used during their spells, rituals, and ceremonies.

*If you use water for purification you can use water you have left out in a container during a full moon, so it becomes charged with the moon's energy.

Religion: A set of beliefs that usually honors a higher power.

Religious Witch: A Religious Witch may follow a religion in accordance with her witchcraft practices.

Ritual: A ritual is a ceremony that is generally done the same way all the time. Rituals are done during particular events such as Sabbats, or even moon phases. Rituals Are beneficial because they help you in being consistent in the craft.

Ritual Ceremony: A ceremony performed to achieve desired effects, where your spell work is practiced.

Ritual Tools: The tools used to accomplish your desired effects from the ritual or spell you are accomplishing.

Rod: A rod is a wand, stick, staff, or even metal that is straight and is used in spell work. Rods are also used in divining.

*I use a carved walking stick that belonged to my father when I need a rod.

Sabbat: The Sabbats are special holidays. Generally, there are four or eight Sabbats that are celebrated throughout the year. The four main Sabbats are Samhain, Yule (the winter solstice), Imbolc, Ostara, Beltane, Litha (the summer solstice), Lammas, and Mabon (the autumnal equinox). Each Sabbat is a holiday, a feast day and a celebration day.

Sachet: Sachets are small cloth bags that contain herbs, spices, talismans, and or amulets that are made and used for spell work. They can be used for protection, attraction, or banishing. Sachet bags can be made out of many materials and colors. They can be solid or made from netting. The materials you use to fill the sachet bags should be in accordance with your spells. For example, if you are carrying a sachet bag to attract money, it should be gold or green, and you may want to put coins in it.

Sacred Space: Your sacred space is the space you have set aside for your craft. It can be indoors or outdoors. It doesn't have to be an entire room; it may be a corner where you place your altar. If you choose not to have a sacred space, that's alright as well. I have an area in my home-office where I keep my tools. But I do the majority of my rituals and spells outdoors on my patio in my backyard. The important thing to remember is that whenever you do rituals or spell work, you will need to purify and charge your space.

Samhain: The Sabbat celebrated around November first and considered the first day of Winter.

Scrying: Scrying is accomplished by using tools such as crystal balls. You meditate, then gaze into the crystal ball to see visions of past or future events. Some people use water and glass as well as crystal. It is a form of divining.

Scrying Mirror: A mirror may be used for scrying. It can be a reflective mirror or a black mirror. You use a scrying mirror the same way you use a crystal ball. You may see images in the mirror from the past or future. It is a form of divining.

*I have a tortoise shell mirror that belonged to my mother that I use for scrying.

Sea Witch: Sea Witches are drawn to Water. Sea Witches focus on moon lore and the ebb and flow of the tide. They are attuned to the weather in their practice.

Seed Moon: April full moon.

Shaman: Shamans are able to alter their state-of-mind and work from that altered state. They are able to communicate on the spiritual realm when in trance. They work with divination and healing and can channel messages.

Shielding: Shielding techniques are used to protect yourself or others from negative energy by creating a barrier to block the negativity.

Sigil: A sigil is a drawn symbol used in spell work. Sigils represent prosperity, money, love, protection, and a host of other conditions. You may carry a sigil with you the same way you would an amulet or a talisman. You can find sigils online, but here again I believe the ones you create yourself are more effective because of the energy you are putting into the creation as you work. Sigils may be used as your signature on letters, emails, and cards. You can also create a special sigil for your altar.

Smoke cleansing: Smoke cleansing is accomplished by using incense, or herbs. It is a purification process.

Smudge: Smudging is another purification process. You use a smudge stick to cleanse your home or even your body of negative or unwanted energy. I smudge with sage monthly, or when I feel negative energy in my home.

Snow Moon: November full moon.

Solar Eclipse: A solar eclipse occurs at the time of the new moon. The moon passes between the earth and the sun blocking the sun. There are total and partial eclipses.

Solitary Witch: A solitary is a witch who works alone. She does not belong to any group.

Solstice: A solstice occurs twice a year. There is a summer and a winter solstice. The summer solstice is the longest day of the year with sunlight. The winter solstice is the shortest day of the year to receive sunlight. At the time of the summer solstice the sun has moved to its highest point in the sky just as in the winter it is the lowest point in the sky (from the horizon).

Spell: A spell is something that is cast to bring about something desired, material, spiritual, or a condition. Spells are focused energy. Spells are written and or spoken words. Speaking your spell aloud is important especially when it is repeated in a meditative state. You can chant your spell as many times as you feel necessary, you will know when you are finished. I write my own spells in four-line rhymes because this is what works for me. Four-line rhymes are easy to remember and chant. They also tend to become like a song when I am chanting them, and I believe that adds more energy to what I am attempting to achieve. It is important to remember to do your spells with focused intent. Your intent is what drives your spell.

Spell Craft: Spell craft is the craft of writing, and casting spells. Again, you may create your own spells, or use spells you've read in books or online. I believe that crafting my own spells and crafting my own materials I use in my magic work gives my work more power.

Spirit: Spirit is non-physical. It is of higher consciousness. It is the top point of the pentagram where all the forces come together. In religion spirit is all there is. In a human spirit is the essence, the energy, we are spirit in a physical human body. The body ceases to exist but spirit lives on.

Spirit Animal: A spirit animal is an animal claimed by a human to be their guide. It is the essence of the animal. For example, a tiger may be your spirit animal. If so, you as the human exude the essence of a tiger.

Spirit world: Wiccans, witches, practitioners of magic generally accept the spirit world as real. They usually accept an afterlife and have no problem contacting the spirit world.

Stang: A tree or a forked branch used during rituals or on an altar.

Statement of Intent: A statement of intent is the spoken purpose of a spell. A spell begins with a statement of intent. The intent is the power behind the spell. The stronger the intent, the stronger the spell will be. A statement of intent is generally a positive statement. The very foundation of spell work begins with a statement of intent by the person performing the spell.

Storm Moon: February full moon.

Subconscious Mind: The subconscious mind is the part of the mind that functions below the conscious mind.

Summerland: Where the body goes to rest in Paganism. Also known as the land of the dead.

Supermoon: A supermoon is used to describe a full or new moon that occurs when the moon is in the closest position to the Earth. A supermoon happens from three to five times a year.

Sword: A sword is a tool used to direct energy. It is similar to using a wand, or a staff. Again, the energy it wields is the energy you, the practitioner put into it, you must charge the sword the same way you would charge any tool you use in your craft.

Sympathetic Magic: Like attracts like, used in spell work to accomplish your intent.

Taglock: An item used in spell. Something that links to the spell. In a banishing spell you may use something that belongs to the person you are banishing as part of the spell. If you were to write the person's name on paper, you might fold something into the paper and then burn it as you say your incantation that banishes the person from your life. *See banishing.

Talisman: A talisman is an object that the user believes holds magical properties that bring good luck to the possessor or protect the possessor from evil or harm. A talisman usually has to be charged to hold magical powers. A talisman may be worn, carried in a mojo bag, placed on an altar, or brought out during spell work.

Thoughtform: Thoughtforms are bundles of psychic energy created by a magic practitioner to work for them.

Threefold Law: The rule of three basically states that whatever energy a person puts forth whether negative or positive will come back to that person in threes. Think of it as karma three times.

Tincture: A tincture is made using some type of alcohol and herbs. You can make your own tinctures using herbs and any type of alcohol preferably 100 proof such as Everclear or vodka. I use Everclear for my tinctures. Place your herb (your choice) in a mason jar, then pour the Everclear (or alcohol of choice) in the jar, and seal it. I let my tinctures sit for a year before opening the jar. When you do open the jar, strain the mixture into a clean jar, and seal again. Tinctures can be taken under the tongue (internally). General a few drops are all that is necessary. If you are going to make and use tinctures, be sure to get more information on what herbs are used for what specific purposes.

Traditional Witch: A Traditional Witch who is Wiccan focuses her practice on her religion.

Uncrossing: Uncrossing is simply removing a curse that has been thrust upon you. You can also use binding and banishing to remove curses.

U: Universe

Vernal Equinox: The vernal equinox is the Spring equinox. It occurs around the twenty first of March.

Visualization: Visualization is the process of forming mental images in your mind. You can also make visualization boards of what you want by cutting pictures and sayings from magazines and pasting them on a board, or cardboard, and meditating on the board for a period of time. People use visualization for creating their world the way they would like it to be. You can use visualization during your spell work instead of chanting.

Voodoo doll: A Voodoo doll is a poppet or effigy used in magic. To some this type of magic is negative. I create and use my own dolls for specific purposes. Voodoo dolls can be a tool for focus when using them in spell work. They can represent people, situations, or desires. I find by using a voodoo doll my intent and focus are sharp.

Wand: A wand is a rod, or a stick, that is used as a tool in your magic. I created my own wand using a cinnamon stick, feathers, yarn, and trinkets that were personal to me. You can create different wands that are used for a variety of reasons. My wand is used for prosperity spells.

Waning Moon: The waning moon is the time when the moon appears to become smaller. The waning moon is a time for decrease and elimination. This is a time to do spell work when you want to eliminate something or someone from your life.

Waxing Moon: The waxing moon is the time when the moon appears to grow in the sky, when it is most visible. The waxing moon is a time for increase and gain. refers to the application of wax on something. Your spell work during the waxing moon would be for situations of gain and increase.

Wheel of the Year: The wheel of the year in Wicca, is a full cycle of each of the four seasons that make up a year.

White Witch: White witches practice goodness and benevolence in all they do. They do not cast spells that cause harm. They do not practice any type of selfish magic. White Witches live their life by the Wiccan Rede.

Wicca: Wicca is a religious practice where magic and spell-work are used, but it is not all about magic and spell-work. Wicca has been around throughout recorded history but wasn't always called Wicca. Wicca is nature oriented and considered a religion. Witchcraft and witches are usually associated with Wicca, but not all Wiccans practice witchcraft and not all witches are Wiccan. Wicca has a set of beliefs, and certain holidays it celebrates.

Wiccan: Wiccan is an individual that belongs to the religion called Wicca. Or, it can be used to describe anything related to Wicca, spells, spell work, talismans, objects, rituals, etc.

Wiccan Rede: "And harm ye none, do what ye will."

Widdershins: Moving counterclockwise when performing rituals.

Witch: Generally, a witch is female. A witch is usually associated with the practice of witchcraft. Witches are not necessarily Pagan, or Wiccan, but they certainly can practice both. They can also be Christian or associated with any religious belief. A group of witches who practice together are generally members of a coven. A solitary witch practices alone, and is not usually a member of a group, or coven. Their practice is usually done in and around their home. An eclectic witch does not follow a specific tradition and is not initiated into a coven. It is a more modern way to practice. Eclectic witches are not near as formal as witches in a coven. Eclectic witches create their own methods, spells, chants, affirmations, incantations, and rituals. But they don't necessarily turn away from traditional tried-and-true methods either. Eclectic witches follow their own path; they create their own magic. They may follow a tradition but aren't bothered if they don't. Most witches follow and use the basics of witchcraft, such as moon charts for spells, candles, herbs, spices, oils, and trinkets.

Witch Doctor: A witch doctor creates his own natural medicines for healing. Witch doctors are deeply spiritual and have a serious respect for nature.

Witchcraft: Witchcraft is a practice, that has a formal set of beliefs. Some people disagree with witchcraft as a religion and call it a set of skills used to practice magic.

Wolf Moon: January full moon.

Yule: The Sabbat celebrated as the Winter solstice around December twenty-first.

Yule Log: The log (legend says use oak) that is burned on Yule.

As you become familiar with this glossary of Wiccan terms, you might check some online sources for more in-depth terms to build your knowledge. The more you learn, the more powerful your magic will become. And by studying and broadening your horizons, you are, in effect practicing the craft. You might set your sights on learning something new every day. The more you know, the more you know!

Incantation Glossary

From my first book of this 'beginner' series, I have repeatedly told you rhyming ditties work best for me. They are sort of like repeating the invocations used with Rosaries and Mala beads. I, in fact, use both because I am a hands-on person. Visualization is not my forte! I don't use my Rosary or Mala beads when practicing the craft, but I do use them as a sort of talisman when I am trying to center myself and nothing else is working.

Anyway, all of that aside, I am including a chapter with my rhyming ditties in the beginner books. As you read through these invocations, you can see that they may be inter-changeable.

As I go forward with these books, I will add to this chapter much the same as I add to the glossary.

Please, if any of my invocations work for you, feel free to incorporate them into your work. Or try writing your own. You'd be surprised what you can come up with, and there is something about an accomplishment that makes life just a little bit sweeter!

From Book of Shadows

Talisman charge and blessing (Whatever I am
blessing goes in the blank, it could be a crystal,
a wand, a rock, oil, or whatever I have created)

I bless this _____ to the powers
that be
all good things now work through me.
Blessed be.

Release someone, a condition, or a situation.

I release _____ to their—its highest
good,
they—it goes their way, and I go my way,
and we are free of each other, and karmic debt.
Blessed be.

House Mortgage

To pay in full
By my magic
I bless this home and everything it holds
Bring me the money, the finance, the means
To own my home on my own.
Blessed be

Immediate need (I use this frequently
throughout the day as it pops into my mind.)

Money, money comes to me
It is my will, so it must be.
Blessed be.

Lottery (I play the lottery. I say this when I purchase my ticket. Don't forget to bless your tickets to the power of luck and chance!)

Money, money comes to me
I have won the lottery
Blessed be

Money (For whatever purpose you have in mind)

Money, money blessed be
Bring wealth and riches straight to me
Blessed be

Prosperity (Prosperity is not just money, people prosper in a lot of diverse ways)

Prosperity, prosperity
Find your way to me
Prosperity, prosperity
Bring all that I can see
Blessed be

Extra money for your personal use

A dollar here, a dollar there,

I see dollars everywhere
Make your way into my home
Stay awhile, do not roam
Blessed be

A specific amount you need (a hundred, a thousand, you fill in the amount)

A hundred here, a hundred there
I see money everywhere
Bring my hundreds straight to me
As I need, so it must be
Blessed be

Soul mate (Her can be substituted for him)

Lovely lady of the moon
Bring my soul mate
And bring him soon.
Blessed be.

Family love

The candle burns and lights the way
For family coming home to stay
Blessed be

Friends

Fill my life with friends untold
All that I desire

My world can hold
Blessed be

World (he and brother are not gender specific)

May the world be enfolded in love
From earth below to the heavens above
May all mankind accept one another
Treat everyone like he is your brother
Blessed be

Specific condition (You can put any condition where I put cancer, since I am a cancer survivor, I used cancer)

Hear my plea to the powers that be
Keep my body cancer free
Blessed be.

General

Keep my body healthy and strong
Keep my lifeline forever long
Keep me free from harm and fear
Keep peace and love abiding here
Blessed be.

Success
Success in all I want and need
Comes through my door today

Success in what I want to be
Shines through in all I say.
Blessed be

Happiness

Happiness comes to my life
Be gone anger, stress and fear
I am happy, and free from strife
Negativity can't come near
Blessed be

Rejuvenating happiness

Lovely lady of the moon
Take away my pain
Lovely lady of the moon
Make me happy once again
Blessed be

Everything spell (I desire)

Success beyond my wildest dreams
Wealth beyond my wildest schemes
Love and health fulfilled desires
My life becomes all I aspire
Blessed be

From Moon Phase Rituals Made Easy

Luna Luna work with me
Show me what I need to see
Bring to light what I might do
So, I may be blessed like you.
Blessed be

Moon of darkness
Moon of light
Help me find
My way tonight
Blessed be

Mother moon shining bright
Help me see my way tonight
Share your power, strength, and light
Make it happen, make it right
Blessed be

Lovely Luna rising high
Lighting up the nighttime sky
Remove my barriers, darkness, and pain
Make my life grow light again
Blessed be

Oh, bright and silvery moon on high
Lighting up the nighttime sky
Fill my life with riches untold

All you deliver I can hold
Blessed be

From Sabats and Esbats Made Easy

Spells of **Imbolc** can focus on cleansing the home, spirit, and body, include love in these spells.

May the powers that be bless this home
Making it sacred, pure and clean
Let nothing but love, joy and happiness
Enter by sights and forces unseen
Blessed be

Spells of **Ostara** can focus on the arrival of Spring, rebirth, new beginnings, and fertility.

Blessings of newness and fertility abound
Making the environment lush
Let nothing but balance, hope, and renewal
Light up the days and the nights.
Blessed be

Spells of **Beltane** can focus on the beginning of the planting season.

Bless this ground by the Powers that be
So the seeds of my spirit can grow
Let nothing negative block my way
So my words of power don't sway.
Blessed be

Spells of **Litha** revolve around the Summer Solstice and the longest day and shortest night of the year.

Bless this day the Powers that be
Let our time be joyous and filled with play
Set our spirits free to fly high and wide
As we thank you for blessings, we abide
Blessed be

Spells of **Lammas** revolve around the first harvest of the Summer.

Bless this day the Powers that be
Let our time be joyous and filled with play
Set our spirits free to fly high and wide
As we thank you for blessings, we abide
Blessed be

Spells of **Mabon**, Autumn has arrived. Daylight is waning, and it's getting darker earlier.

Bless this time as the colors change
The season is rich, in bounty and beauty
Lay all negativity aside
By the power of three abide.
Blessed be

Spells for **Samhain** can revolve around your connection to people and the environment.

Spirits protect me and those I love
Both here and now and in between
Keep my spirit alive and well
And bless the house in which I dwell.
Blessed be

Spells of **Yule**. Center your spells and incantations around home and hearth. Family and friends are important now.

Lords and ladies and powers that be
Bless my home, my friends and family.
The season is joyous, and I am well
By the power of three in my heart please dwell.
Blessed be

From Banishing, Binding, Cursing, and Hexing

I **banish** _____ *(name of person)*
You brought discord into my life
And caused me turmoil and pain
My life holds no place for you
You will never affect me again.
Blessed be

I **banish** _____ *(a condition or situation)*
My life has no room for you
Release your hold on me
Move on, be gone, withdraw, depart
As I begin anew and restart.
Blessed be

I **bind** _____ *(insert name)*
You will never cross my path again
Or cause me hurt and pain
I bind you left, I bind you right,
You're gone forever more.
Blessed be

I **bind** _____ *(a condition or situation)*
I bind you today, I bind you tonight
I bind you left; I bind you right.
I bind you tight, no more to be,
I bind you gone away from me.

Blessed be.

I **bind** _____ *(behavior)*
I bind your conduct,
It stops today
Hear me, don't test me
Or I'll send you away.
Blessed be.

I **curse** *you* _____ *(name or*
condition)
I curse you here, I curse you now
I curse you forever more
Stay away from me and mine
For I now close that door.
Blessed be

I **hex** _____ (fill in the person
or condition)
I cast this hex upon you
You shall endure all that you have placed on me
I cast this hex upon you
You shall never more be free.
Blessed be

I **hex** *you* _____ *(name or*
condition)
May you forever suffer what you brought upon me
May you never know how my pain felt

May all your days be burdened
With what you have dealt.
Blessed be.

Reminder

PLEASE remember, there is no right or wrong way to perform your rituals and spells. Magic is personal, and what works for some may not work for others. By all means, attempt the tried and true methods but don't be afraid to add your own personal touch to your craft. If something feels right, it is usually right. Similarly, if something feels wrong, it is generally wrong.

I am happy to share what works for me, and if it works for you, so much the better. The keywords to remember are **concentration, regularity, intent, focus,** and **purpose.** Solitary and eclectic witches will perform their magic differently than covens. It is still magic.

Finally

If you are new to the craft, just beginning your journey, try to use very basic techniques, so you don't become frustrated if things don't turn out the way you want them to.

Different magic practitioners, witches, or witchcraft traditions will practice using banishing, binding, cursing, and hexing in accordance with their own ways. Or, they may be against these practices because they are manipulative magic, even black magic.

If you are a part of a particular coven, group, circle, gathering, or tradition, you should look into the practice they use and follow through with that tradition.

Permission, understanding, and intent are key words when using magic. Intent is powerful because if your intent is not strong, your magic will not be strong. Your intent must be spot on for magic to work. I believe most people who work with magic fully understand the outcomes and consequences. However, with black magic, the receiver may not understand what is happening to him. Here again, under certain circumstances, I have no problem with this because there is no help for some people and in those cases, you must do what you must do. So long as you protect yourself and understand there may be consequences, I don't see a problem. I banish, bind, curse, and hex when I must.

When repeating incantations in your circle or at your altar, repeat them as often as necessary until you *feel* your energy and power changing and growing.

Practice, practice, practice! And, log your journey. When you find your niche, you will know you are home.

Finally, when you become adept at working with banishing, binding, cursing, and hexing, use it wisely, and sparingly, and as a last resort.

Prologue

Coming soon from E.M. Fairchilde

What kind of witch are you¿

Made in the USA
Las Vegas, NV
17 June 2022

50382183R00073